Just Joking 4

NATIONAL GEOGRAPHIC KiDS

300 hilarious jokes about everything, including tongue twisters, riddles, **and more!**

by Rosie Gowsell Pattison

NATIONAL GEOGRAPHIC

WASHINGTON, D.C.

KNOCK, KNOCK.

Who's there?
Emma.
Emma who?
Emma going to the store,
do you need anything?

4

HA!HA!
HA!HA!HA!
HA!HA!HA!
HA!HA!HA!HA!
HA!HA!HA!HA!
HA!HA!HA!HA!
HA!HA!HA!
HA!HA!

The bearded dragon
gets its name from
the row of spiny
scales around its
throat and neck.

5

Despite their size, hippos can outrun most humans.

KNOCK, KNOCK.

Who's there?
Alpaca.
Alpaca who?
Alpaca sweater for you in case it gets cold.

Say this fast three times:

Sam sat sipping
soda silently.

Q How long did
the hamster
work out?

A For a wheelie long time.

7

Say this fast three times:

Are our oranges ordered?

Q What do pigs wear on their feet when it's cold out?

A Oinkle socks.

Q What kind of movies do baby chickens watch?

A Chick flicks.

Q Why did the **rapper** carry an **umbrella?**

A Fo' drizzle!

8

Each of a tarsier's eyeballs is larger than its brain!

KNOCK, KNOCK.

Who's there?
Berry.
Berry who?
Berry nice to see you again.

KNOCK, KNOCK.

Who's there?
Knee.
Knee who?
Knee to come in,
it's cold out here!

A group of turtles
is called a bale.

Q Why did the slice of bread stay home from school?

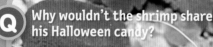

A It was feeling crumby.

Q Why wouldn't the shrimp share his Halloween candy?

A Because he was a little shellfish.

KNOCK,
KNOCK.

Who's there?
Tuna.
Tuna who?
Tuna the TV, my show is starting!

Chimpanzees are our closest relative—we share 98 percent of the same DNA!

Why did the dachshund put ketchup on himself?

Because someone called him a hot dog!

Say this fast three times:

Zucchinis in bikinis.

Q

What did the **nose** say to the **cold?**

A Catch ya later!

Q How do you stop a charging rhinoceros?

A Take away his credit card.

Q What kind of cell phone does an optometrist use?

A An eye phone.

15

TONGUE TWISTER!

Say this fast three times:

Slippery slimy slithering snakes slide sideways sometimes.

KNOCK, KNOCK.

Who's there?
Minnow.
Minnow who?
Let minnow when
I can come in!

Seagulls can drink salt water!
Special glands flush out the
salt. It is then forced out of
openings in their beaks.

Q What do you call a **dog who talks a lot?**

A A blabrador.

TONGUE TWISTER!

Say this fast three times:

A real rare railroad.

Q Why did the mushroom get invited to so many parties?

A Because he was a fungi!

Q Why do ghosts like to ride in **elevators?**

A Because it lifts their spirits.

Q What do you call a laughing rodent?

A A giddy pig.

Q Why didn't the butcher join the poker game?

A Because the steaks were too high.

KNOCK, KNOCK.

Who's there?
Lettuce.
Lettuce who?
Lettuce in, we have to finish dressing.

A tiger can eat up to 70 pounds (32 kg) of meat in one meal.

Red pandas clean their
fur like cats — by
licking themselves!

KNOCK,

KNOCK.

Who's there?
Turnip.
Turnip who?
Turnip the heat.
It's freezing
in here!

Cows can drink up to 35 gallons (132 L) of water and eat up to 50 pounds (23 kg) of food every day!

KNOCK,

KNOCK.

Who's there?
Julian.
Julian who?
Just Julian, there is no one else with me.

24

Q How did the flashlight feel when its batteries died?

A It was delighted.

Q Why are **horses** so **calm** under pressure?

A Because they come from a stable environment.

Q Why can't snails play nicely together?

A Because they always slug each other.

Q Why do geologists make the best guitarists?

A Because they know how to rock!

25

Q What is a **duck's** favorite **junk food?**

A Quacker-Jacks.

Q Why did the deer need braces?

A Because he had buck teeth.

Q What kinds of **mistakes** are common in a **blood bank?**

A Type-Os.

Q Why are elephants always headed to the pool?

A Because they always have their trunks on.

Cats use their whiskers to "feel" whether they will fit into a space they are entering.

KNOCK, KNOCK.

Who's there?
Noah.
Noah who?
Noah good place for dinner? I'm starving!

What did the **sea lion** think of his new home?

He gave it a seal of approval.

KNOCK,
KNOCK.

Who's there?
Arrrrr.
Arrrrr who?
Arrrr ya' comin' to the pirate party, matey?

Llamas are plant-eaters known as herbivores. Their stomachs have three compartments and they chew their cud like cattle do.

Q

Why do **zombies** make good **musicians?**

Because they are always decomposing.

A

Q What kind of cookie takes martial arts classes?

A A ninja-bread cookie.

Q What did the ape order for lunch?

A A gorilla-cheese sandwich.

Q How did the mummy get to class?

A On the ghoul bus.

Q What did the snake do when he didn't get his own way?

A He threw a hissy fit.

Q Why didn't the **melon** run away to get **married?**

A Because it cantaloupe.

Ring-tailed lemurs have a scent gland on their tails that they rub against trees. It leaves a smelly mark to tell other lemurs where they've been!

KNOCK, KNOCK.

Who's there?
Macaw.
Macaw who?
Macaw won't start. Can I use your phone?

KNOCK, KNOCK.

Who's there?
Hugo.
Hugo who?
Hugo to the store
and I'll stay home.

Known for their slowness, two-toed sloths live in trees. They spend a lot of their time sleeping.

Why didn't the **wild pig** get invited to the **party?**

Because he's BOAR-ing!

MARIE:
Did you cut the grass today?

GARY:
No, I just didn't feel mow-tivated.

Q What kind of fruit should you call if you lock yourself out of the house?

A A key-wi.

Q What do you get if you cross an igloo and a kitten?

A An eski-meow.

TONGUE TWISTER!

Say this fast three times:

Rosie runs rapidly in the rain.

Q What do you get when you cross a scientist and a dog?

A A laboratory retriever.

Q

What do you get when you cross a **sheepdog** and a **rose?**

A A collie-flower.

HA! HA! HA! HA! HA! HA! HA! HA! HA!

HA! HA! HA! HA! HA! HA! HA! HA! HA! HA!

KNOCK, KNOCK.

Who's there?
Iguana.
Iguana who?
Iguana stop in and say hello.

Snowy owls are silent hunters. They sit and wait for their prey, then pounce and eat it whole.

Mark the

went to

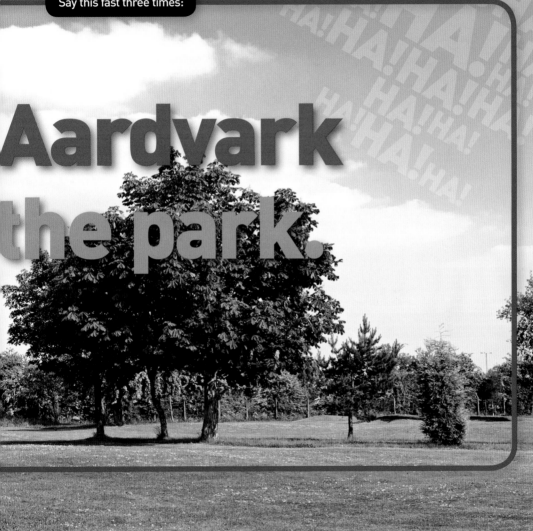

Aardvark the park.

HA! HA! HA! HA! HA! HA! HA! HA! HA! HA! HA! HA! HA! HA! HA!

A tiger's stripes are like fingerprints! No two tigers have the same stripe pattern.

Why is a tiger big, orange, and striped?

Because if it was small, smooth, and red it would be an apple.

Q Where do penguins keep their money?

A In a snow bank.

Q How do french fries get to work?

A On their fry-cycles.

Male deer:
Oh no, we will never get home now!

Female deer:
Why don't we keep going?

Male deer:
Because the buck stops here.

KNOCK, KNOCK.

Who's there?
Art.
Art who?
Art you going to open this door?

Chameleons can change color quickly depending on their health, mood, or temperature.

Q What do rabbits do when they get hot?

A Turn on their hare-conditioning.

Q

What kind of **dancing** happens in the **sink?**

Tap dancing.

A

HA! HA! HA! HA! HA! HA! HA!

45

KNOCK,

KNOCK.

Who's there?
Doughnut.
Doughnut who?
I doughnut belong
here. I must have the
wrong address.

Lions can sleep for up
to 20 hours a day!

HA! HA! HA! HA! HA! HA! HA! HA! HA! HA! HA! HA! HA! HA! HA! HA! HA! HA!

Q Why did the hot dog lose the race?

A Because he couldn't ketchup. But don't worry, he mustard the strength to try again!

Q What do you call an angry pig?

A Dis-gruntled

Q Why did the **watch** need a **vacation?**

A Because it was all wound up.

FUNNY PUNS

The new shark display at the zoo was Jawesome!

What do you call a **sheep** that can **sing** and **dance?**

Lady Baa Baa.

49

Green frogs can live for up to ten years!

KNOCK, KNOCK.

Who's there?
Santa.
Santa who?
Santa card to you last week, did you get it yet?

Q What do you get if you teach a spotted cat to sing?

A A show leopard.

Q What oinks and tells you the weather forecast?

A A ham radio.

Q What kind of dinosaur could do magic?

A A Tyrannosaurus hex.

Q Why won't the baker share his bread recipe with anyone?

A He says it is on a knead-to-know basis.

51

Bloodhounds are built for smelling! Their long, droopy ears help trap scents and their extra-large nasal cavities help process them.

What type of dog does dracula own?

Little Biter

A bloodhound.

Brown bears are omnivorous, which means they eat both plants and animals.

KNOCK, KNOCK.

Who's there?
Ida.
Ida who?
Ida hard time finding this house.

54

Q What do you call a piece of fruit that needs glasses?

A Visually im-peared.

Q

What can slither and fly?

A A feather boa.

Q What **sparkles** and hops?

A A Kanga-ruby.

Say this fast three times:

Valerie's hourly salary.

Q What do you get if you cross a **van** and an **elephant?**

A A vehicle with extra trunk space.

Q What kind of food should you eat at the seashore?

A Pier-ogies.

What do you call a
pig from
Ontario?

Canadian bacon.

KNOCK, KNOCK.

Who's there?
Scott.
Scott who?
Scott nothing to do.
I'm bored.

Don't make fun of this guy's nose!
The strange-nosed chameleon has
the sharpest teeth and longest
claws of any chameleon.

I'll take mine to go! Mandrills have large pockets in their cheeks that they stuff with food to eat at a later time.

KNOCK, KNOCK.

Who's there?
Ivanna.
Ivanna who?
Ivanna go for a pizza, care to join me?

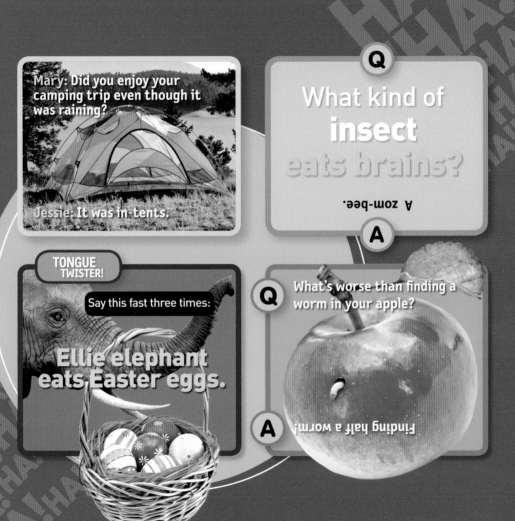

Mary: Did you enjoy your camping trip even though it was raining?

Jessie: It was in-tents.

Q

What kind of **insect** eats brains?

A zom-bee.

A

TONGUE TWISTER!

Say this fast three times:

Ellie elephant eats Easter eggs.

Q What's worse than finding a worm in your apple?

A Finding half a worm!

61

What does a **ghostly magician** say when he does a trick?

A Abra-cadaver.

TONGUE TWISTER!

Say this fast three times:

Big fat flat black cat.

A pelican uses the pouch under its bill to scoop up fish.

KNOCK, KNOCK.

Who's there?
Sapphires.
Sapphires who?
Sapphires started.
Let's make s'mores!

63

What do you call a turtle wearing a scarf?

Cold.

Box turtles are omnivores. They eat snails, insects, vegetation, and fruit. They have even been known to snack on dead animals!

65

HA!HA!HA!HA!HA!HA!HA!HA!HA!HA!HA!

KNOCK,

KNOCK.

Who's there?
Vadar.
Vadar who?
Vadar, there's a fly
in my soup.

If a mother red kite eagle
senses danger, she will signal
her hatchlings to play dead
until the coast is clear.

Say this fast three times:

Gigantic gourds grew in Gracie's garden.

Q How many jugglers does it take to screw in a light bulb?

A One, but it takes three light bulbs.

67

Q

What is a **dentist's** favorite animal?

A

A molar bear.

CUSTOMER: So do you like being a baker?

BAKER: Sure do, it's a piece of cake!

Q Why are pie makers so well prepared?

A Because they always have a flan B.

Q Does it cost a lot of money to buy an insect?

A Not if they're free-bees!

SALE

68

Say this fast three times:

Five fearless firefighters finally finished the fondue.

The dark areas around a meerkat's eyes work as built-in sunglasses to reduce the sun's glare on its face.

KNOCK, KNOCK.

Who's there?
Gnome.
Gnome who?
There's no place like gnome.

DINER: Waiter, why are there ducks swimming in my dinner?

WAITER: I thought you asked for quackers in your soup.

Q

Why doesn't corn like Halloween?

A They think it's ear-y.

Q What kind of dog cries all the time?

A A Chi-waa-waa.

71

The spectacled caiman is a smaller species of crocodile. They get their name from the bony ridge around their eyes, which makes them look like they're wearing glasses.

KNOCK, KNOCK.

Who's there?
Accordion.
Accordion who?
Accordion to the weather report it is going to rain today.

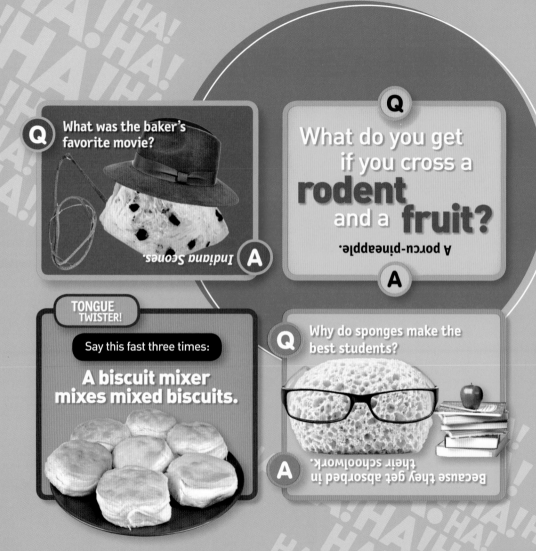

Q What was the baker's favorite movie?

A Indiana Scones.

Q What do you get if you cross a **rodent** and a **fruit?**

A A porcu-pineapple.

TONGUE TWISTER!

Say this fast three times:

A biscuit mixer mixes mixed biscuits.

Q Why do sponges make the best students?

A Because they get absorbed in their schoolwork.

74

What
chews
on trees
and
sings?

Justin Beaver.

Sally's sweets are

Say this fast three times:

super sugary.

In the wild, green tree pythons like to coil around tree branches and rest.

KNOCK, KNOCK.

Who's there?
Cook.
Cook who?
Hey! Who are you calling a cuckoo?

78

Q How do monkeys get down the stairs?

A They slide down the banana-ster.

TONGUE TWISTER!

Say this fast three times:

Silly Sam sat silently for supper.

79

Q How does a bird fix a broken wing?

A With duck tape.

TONGUE TWISTER!

Say this fast three times:

Eddie edited it.

FUNNY PUNS

I quit my job at the **herb garden** because there was too much **over-thyme.**

Q **What has 30 feet and horns?**

A The school band.

The spots on a jaguar's fur are called rosettes.

KNOCK, KNOCK.

Who's there?
Bunny.
Bunny who?
Is some bunny going to let me in?

Horses neigh, or whinny, to communicate with other horses.

KNOCK, KNOCK.

Who's there?
Howard.
Howard who?
Howard I know?

Polar bears have rough pads on their paws that prevent them from slipping when walking on ice.

KNOCK, KNOCK.

Who's there?
Owl.
Owl who?
Owl wait while you get ready.

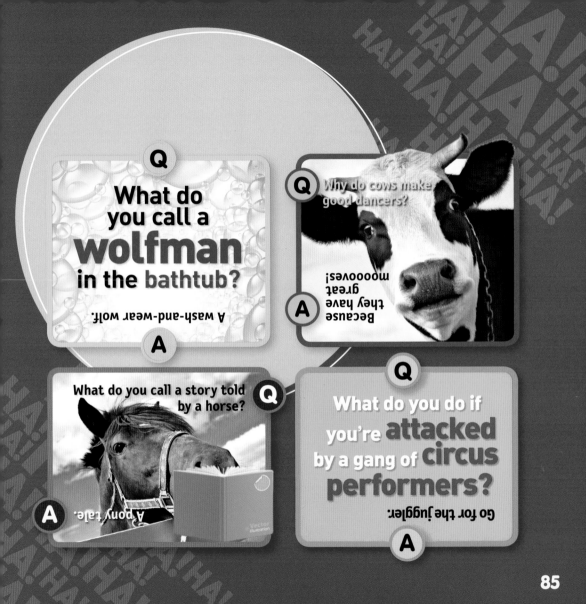

Q

What do you call a wolfman in the bathtub?

A A wash-and-wear wolf.

Q Why do cows make good dancers?

A Because they have great mooooves!

Q What do you call a story told by a horse?

A A pony tale.

Q

What do you do if you're attacked by a gang of circus performers?

A Go for the juggler.

Q Why did the student bring cake to school for his teacher?

A So he could score some brownie points.

Say this fast three times:

Seven sisters sat by the swimming pool.

HA! HA! HA! HA! HA! HA! HA! HA! HA! HA! HA!

KNOCK, KNOCK.

Who's there?
Water.
Water who?
Water you saying?
I don't understand you!

HA! HA! HA! HA! HA! HA! HA! HA! HA!

Dolphins can't breathe through their mouths. They can only breathe through the blowholes on top of their heads.

87

TONGUE TWISTER!

Say this fast three times:

Six thick socks on seven thin sirs.

Polar bears are fantastic swimmers! In Arctic waters they can swim for about 100 miles (161 km) at a time.

What did the
polar bear
order for
lunch?

An iceberg-er.

What do you call a **vegetable** on a **one-wheeled bike?**

A uni-corn.

A

EYE DOCTOR:
Eye see it's time for your appointment.

PATIENT:
Iris you didn't make such a bad pun.

EYE DOCTOR:
Sorry my joke was so cornea.

Q Did you hear about the famous pickle?

He's a really big dill!

A

TONGUE TWISTER!

Say this fast three times:

Big bad bedbugs bite baby boys.

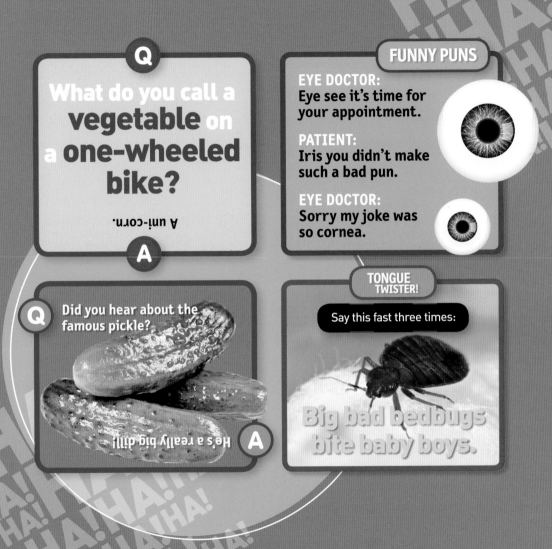

Q **Why did the second chicken cross the road?**

A Because the first chicken forgot her wallet.

Q **What do you call Bigfoot's vegetarian cousin?**

Sas-squash.

A

Q How do you know when owls are excited?

They hoot and holler.

A

92

What do you get if you cross a firecracker with a triceratops?

Dino-mite!

KNOCK,

KNOCK.

Who's there?
Sand.
Sand who?
Sand me a text when you
are ready to leave.

The lionhead goldfish gets its name from
a growth on its head called a wen. It
covers its head, cheeks, and gills.

94

Say this fast three times:

Fuzzy buzzing busy

Bumblebees have two sets of wings, a larger set in the front and a smaller set in the back. They can move them at 130–240 beats per second!

bumblebees.

Baby horses, or foals, can stand up and walk within an hour of being born!

KNOCK, KNOCK.

Who's there?
Colleen.
Colleen who?
Colleen up your room, it's a mess!

Q Why are fireflies like cars?

A Because they both have tail lights.

TONGUE TWISTER!

Say this fast three times:

Eleven elegant elephants ambled into Edinburgh.

Q How long does it take to slip on a peel?

A A bananosecond.

Say this fast three times:

Chop shops stock chops.

Q What kind of shoes do alligators wear?

A Crocs.

Q What did the cannibals serve at their dinner party?

A Finger sandwiches and toe-fu.

A chameleon's tongue is as long as its body.

KNOCK, KNOCK.

Who's there?
Sara.
Sara who?
Sara reason you aren't laughing at my jokes?

101

What happened to the OX who bought his wife chocolates on Valentine's Day?

He became more love-a-bull.

Parrots eat seeds, nuts, and fruit. Some parrots can live for 80 years or more!

KNOCK, KNOCK.

Who's there?
Paul.
Paul who?
Paul up a chair and I will tell you.

Q What do you call a borrowed bison?

A A buffa-loan.

Q Where can you **break** a **board** with your foot and then **sprinkle glitter** on it?

A Martial arts and crafts class.

Q What kind of **dog** loves **Christmas?**

A A pointsetter.

Q What did the deck of cards order for lunch?

A A club sandwich.

FOR RENT

Q What comes from the sea and destroys towns?

A Cod-zilla.

Q What do you call **a vampire** with **a cough?**

A Count Hackula.

Q What did the **bug** say when his **house** burned down?

A "Good thing I have insur-ants."

Q What do you call a cat that gets caught stealing?

A The purr-petrator.

What kind of car does an antelope drive?

An impala.

Domestic geese make great guards! They spread their wings and honk and peck at intruders.

KNOCK, KNOCK.

Who's there?
Alex.
Alex who?
Alex-plain later, just open the door!

Q Why was the student afraid to use his computer?

A Because he didn't want to catch a virus.

TONGUE TWISTER!

Say this fast three times:

The shortstop sports short socks.

KNOCK, KNOCK.

Who's there?
Zucchini.
Zucchini who?
Zucchini doesn't have a last name!

A fox's bushy tail helps it balance. Its tail also makes a warm wrap when it rests.

Q What did one bucket say to the other bucket?

A You look a little pail.

Q What do frogs sit on?

A Toad stools.

KNOCK,
KNOCK.

Who's there?
Rufus.
Rufus who?
Rufus leaking!
Quick get a bucket!

The body slime of
moray eels protects
them against parasites.

What do you get when you cross a lamb and a beetle?

Bah-humbug.

The French bulldog is actually from England! The breed was started to create a smaller type of bulldog.

KNOCK, KNOCK.

Who's there?
Ant.
Ant who?
Ant you glad to see me?

TONGUE TWISTER!

Say this fast three times:

Betty baked big batches of baked beans.

Q What do ghosts put on their bagels?

A Scream cheese.

117

TONGUE TWISTER!

Say this fast three times:

Brady's back bike brake broke.

Q What do you call a deer with one eye?

A No idear!

Q What is it called when *two dinosaurs* bump into one another?

A A tyrannosaurus wreck.

Q Why didn't the bird take a map on his trip?

A He was just winging it.

What did the
fish magician
say to the crowd?

Pick a cod, any cod!

When threatened, the long-spine porcupinefish swallows water to inflate itself. Its spines stick up and make it look scary.

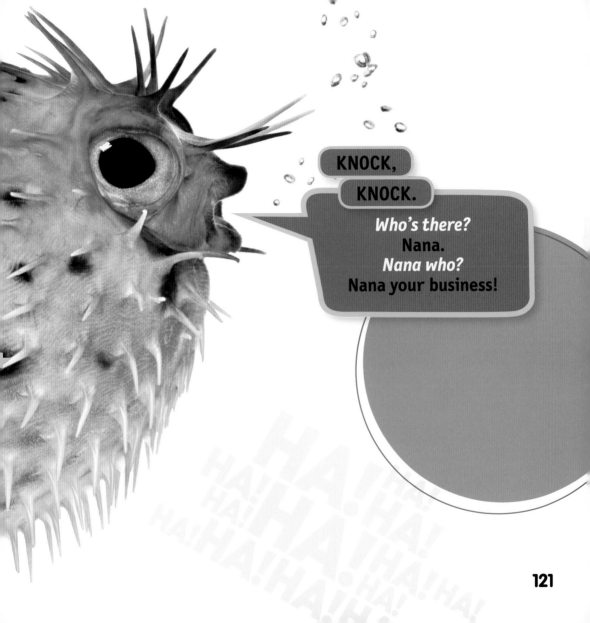

121

KNOCK,

KNOCK.

Who's there?
Stopwatch.
Stopwatch who?
Stopwatch you're doing
and open this door!

There are 21 different types
of macaque monkeys that live
in the world!

MOTHER DOG TO PUPPY:

Did you draw pictures all over the walls?

PUPPY:

I can't help it, I'm a labradoodle!

Q What do you call a pig with a sunburn?

A Bacon.

SUN SCREEN 25 SPF

Q

What do you call **a fish** with no **eye?**

Fsh.

A

Q Why did the pirate go on vacation?

A He needed a little arrr and arrr.

Q What do you call a fish that fixes pianos?

A A tuna fish.

TONGUE TWISTER!

Say this fast three times:

Peppery potato pork pie pudding.

Q What do you call a day without sunshine?

A Night.

Where do **birds** sit at a concert?

In the cheep seats.

125

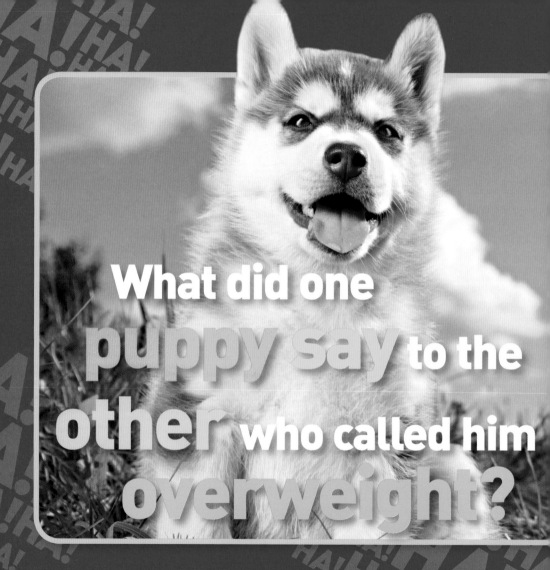

What did one puppy say to the other who called him overweight?

Huskies are strong and full of energy. They were originally bred to pull dogsleds.

"I'm not fat, I'm just a little husky."

Leopard geckos eat their skin after shedding.

KNOCK, KNOCK.

Who's there?
Adore.
Adore who?
Adore closed, but the window is still open.

Q What kind of medication should you give a pig?

A Oink-ment.

TONGUE TWISTER!

Say this fast three times:

Rural juror.

FUNNY PUNS

SHARK: Hey Flipper, you just bumped into me!

FLIPPER: I didn't do it on porpoise but I am dolphinately sorry!

Q What does a dizzy hen lay?

A Scrambled eggs.

Q How is tea served in outer space?

A On flying saucers.

Tasmanian devils got their name from their habit of tearing through food. They have strong jaws and sharp teeth.

KNOCK, KNOCK.

Who's there?
Canoe.
Canoe who?
Canoe help me with my homework?

KNOCK, KNOCK.

Who's there?
Butter.
Butter who?
Butter hurry up, we are going to be late.

The sugar glider is an Australian possum that glides from tree to tree using its loose skin. It eats fruit and nectar.

TONGUE TWISTER!

Say this fast three times:

Henry's horse Horst abhors other horses.

Q What do you call a sick bird with a stealing problem?

A An ill-eagle.

Q What did the cherries do with their treasure?

A They berried it on a desert island.

Q What do you get if you **kiss** a **firecracker?**

A Lipbomb.

Q Why did the eel tour the light bulb factory?

A He thought the experience would be electrifying.

135

Say this fast three times:

Surely Shirley shouldn't shout so shrilly.

Q What kind of crimes do berries commit?

A Strobberies.

HA!HA!HA!
HA!HA!HA!
HA!HA!HA!
HA!HA!HA!

KNOCK, KNOCK.

Who's there?
Police.
Police who?
Police stop telling these corny jokes!

Elephant seals can hold their breath underwater for more than two hours!

137

When do astronauts eat?

At launch time.

HA! HA! HA! HA! HA! HA! HA! HA! HA!

Wild pandas eat mostly just one plant: bamboo!

KNOCK, KNOCK.

Who's there?
Spoon.
Spoon who?
See you spoon!

140

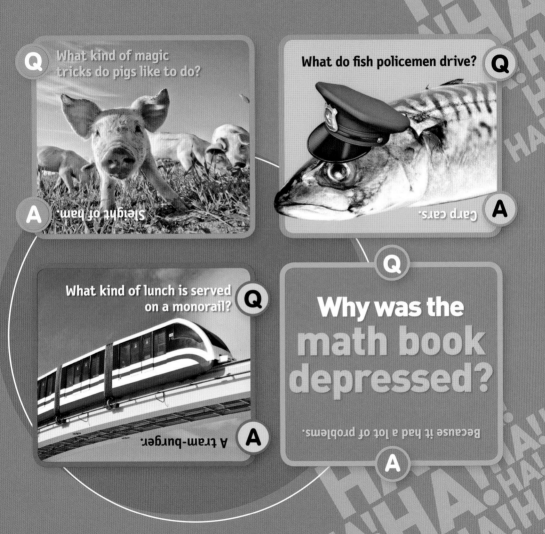

Q What kind of magic tricks do pigs like to do?

A Sleight of ham.

Q What do fish policemen drive?

A Carp cars.

Q What kind of lunch is served on a monorail?

A A tram-burger.

Q Why was the math book depressed?

A Because it had a lot of problems.

141

Q Why didn't Goldilocks eat all of the porridge?

A She thought it was unbearable.

Q What did the salad say to its roommate when invited to a party?

A Lettuce turnip on thyme.

Q Why isn't sea life fun to spend time with?

A Because it can get a little crabby.

Q **What goes crinkle, crinkle, roar?**

A A lion opening a bag of chips.

142

Why should you never hire a marsupial for a job?

Because they aren't koala-fied.

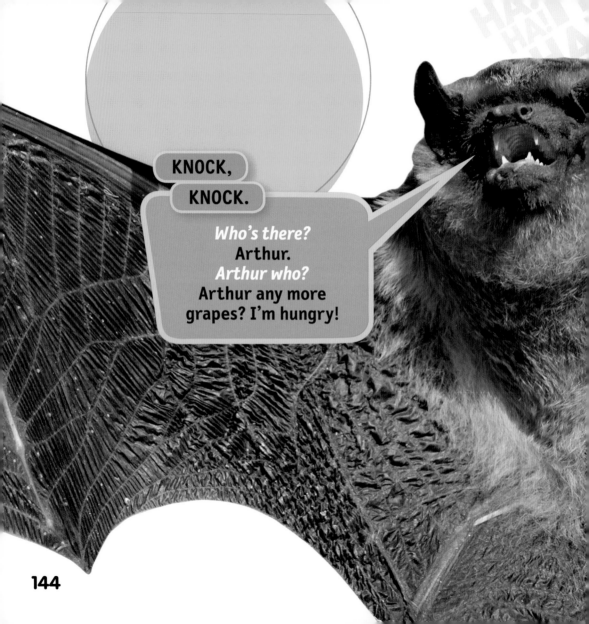

Bat poop, called guano,
is used as plant fertilizer.

Why don't dogs like scary movies?

Because they are terrier-fying.

KNOCK, KNOCK.

Who's there?
Ear.
Ear who?
Ear I am, were you looking for me?

The Chihuahua is the world's smallest dog breed. Most measure 6 to 10 inches (15 to 25 cm) and weigh under 6 pounds (3 kg)!

Say this fast three times:

Toledo was torn by terrible twisters.

Q What do you get if you cross a pastry and a snake?

A A pie-thon.

Q What state serves the smallest drinks?

A Mini-soda.

Q Why did the cow cross the road?

A The chicken had the day off.

Q Which **circus performers** can see in the dark?

A The acro-bats.

TONGUE TWISTER!

Say this fast three times:

A Sasquatch tossed a squash until it was lost.

Why did the sailor put grass on his boat?

He wanted to have a yard sail.

TONGUE TWISTER!

Say this fast three times:

Eleven yellow yodeling yaks grazed gleefully near the glacier.

Camels have long eyelashes that protect their eyes from sand and dust.

KNOCK, KNOCK.

Who's there?
Bacon.
Bacon who?
Whatcha bacon?
It smells great!

Q What kind of animal is good at math?

A A tally-cat.

Q What was the penguin doing on his vacation?

A Nothing, he was just chillin'!

155

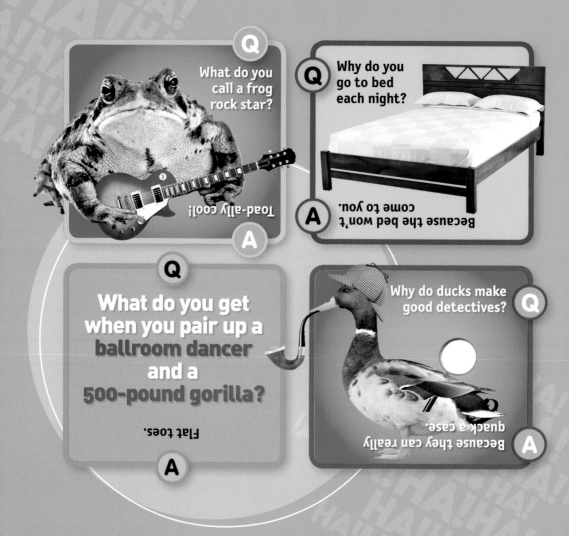

Q What do you call a frog rock star?

A Toad-ally cool!

Q Why do you go to bed each night?

A Because the bed won't come to you.

Q What do you get when you pair up a ballroom dancer and a 500-pound gorilla?

A Flat toes.

Q Why do ducks make good detectives?

A Because they can really quack a case.

156

KNOCK, KNOCK.

Who's there?
Ya.
Ya who?
Yahoo!
Ride 'em cowboy!

Seals use their sensitive whiskers to find food.

158

The Asian small-clawed otter is the smallest otter. It measures from 12 to 24 inches (30 to 61 cm).

TONGUE TWISTER!

Say this fast three times:

Messy mad monkeys make many mistakes.

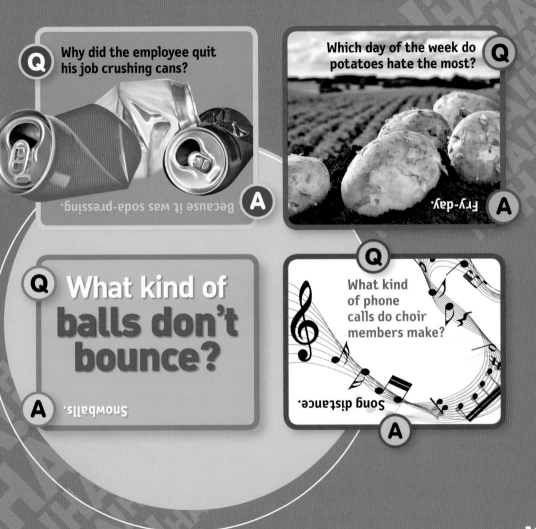

Q Why did the employee quit his job crushing cans?

A Because it was soda-pressing.

Q Which day of the week do potatoes hate the most?

A Fry-day.

Q What kind of **balls don't bounce?**

A Snowballs.

Q What kind of phone calls do choir members make?

A Song distance.

161

Q Why don't owls take good care of their belongings?

A Because they don't give a hoot.

Q How do rabbits send birthday cards?

A By hare-mail.

AIR MAIL

REGISTERED

The emu is a flightless bird. Its powerful legs can run at speeds of up to 31 miles per hour (48 km/h).

KNOCK, KNOCK.

Who's there?
Venice.
Venice who?
Venice dinner?
I'm starving!

163

TONGUE TWISTER!

Say this fast three times:

164

Canoodling poodles like to eat noodles and draw doodles.

Kudus are antelopes native to eastern and southern Africa.

KNOCK, KNOCK.

Who's there?
Sherwood.
Sherwood who?
Sherwood like to come inside.

TONGUE TWISTER!

Say this fast three times:

Christian crushed Christie's crispy chips.

How do you call an elephant? **Q**

A On the ele-phone.

167

KNOCK, KNOCK.

Who's there?
Avenue.
Avenue who?
Avenue heard this joke before?

Ferrets are sound sleepers. They can sleep up to 18 hours a day!

169

Q What is the most **terrifying dinosaur?**

A The scare-o-dactyl.

Q How did the pig get to the hospital?

A By ham-bulance.

Q What do birds do on first dates?

A They go on peck-nics.

Q Why are cattle so good at math?

A Because they use cow-culators.

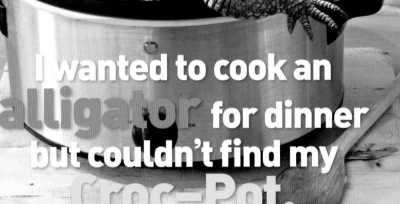

I wanted to cook an alligator for dinner but couldn't find my Croc-Pot.

What do you get if you copy a picture of a mallard?

A repro-duck-tion.

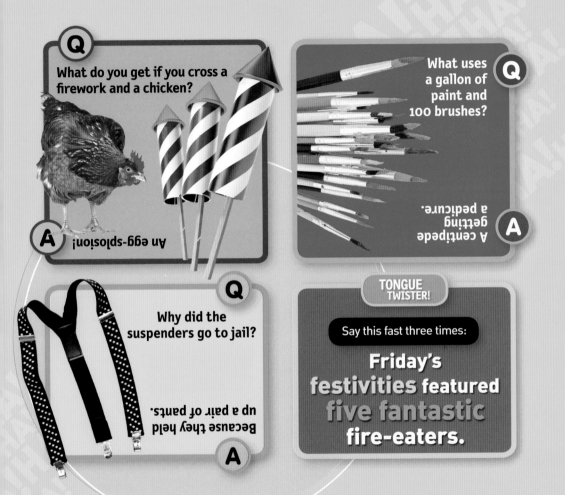

Q

What do you get if you cross a firework and a chicken?

A An egg-splosion!

Q

What uses a gallon of paint and 100 brushes?

A A centipede getting a pedicure.

Q

Why did the suspenders go to jail?

A Because they held up a pair of pants.

TONGUE TWISTER!

Say this fast three times:

Friday's festivities featured five fantastic fire-eaters.

Q Who is a chicken's favorite composer?

A Bach Bach!

Q What is fuzzy and **brown** and goes 90 miles an hour?

A A grizzly bear on a roller coaster.

Q What do cats say when they get hurt?

A "Me-OW!"

Q What do **Santa's helpers** learn in school?

A The elf-abet.

174

KNOCK, KNOCK.

Who's there?
Kitten.
Kitten who?
You gotta be kitten me!

A kookaburra's call sounds like human laughter.

What did the steak sauce say to the steak?

Nice to meat you.

Bulls, and all cattle, are color-blind. Despite popular belief, they're not angered by the color red.

KNOCK, KNOCK.

Who's there?
Mustache.
Mustache who?
I mustache you a question.

Where does water leave its car?

Q

At the water park.

A

How do you throw a party on Jupiter?

Q

You planet.

A

179

Q Why can you trust a hot dog?

A Because it will always be frank with you.

TOM: I bought you this globe for Christmas.

SUE: Thank you, it means the world to me!

Say this fast three times:

Rivers of rainwater ran through the ramparts.

Penguins can't fly but they're excellent swimmers. They use their powerful flippers to propel themselves through water.

KNOCK, KNOCK.

Who's there?
Amal.
Amal who?
Amal ready to go!

KNOCK, KNOCK.

Who's there?
Falafel.
Falafel who?
I falafel, I think
I have the flu.

Bulldogs are famous for snoring. Their short snout, narrow windpipe, and smushed face make it difficult for them to breathe.

TONGUE TWISTER!

Say this fast three times:

An Irish setter in a sweater ate a **pepper** and turned **redder.**

Q

What is the nuttiest letter in the alphabet?

A Cra-Zee.

LEOPARD 1: Can I ask you a question?

LEOPARD 2: Don't put me on the spot!

TONGUE TWISTER!

Say this fast three times:

Real weird rear wheels.

Q

Why don't chickens make good house pets?

A Because they smell fowl.

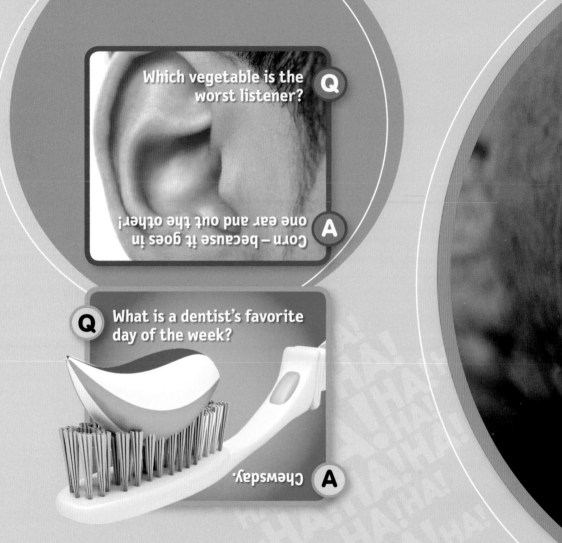

Q Which vegetable is the worst listener?

A Corn — because it goes in one ear and out the other!

Q What is a dentist's favorite day of the week?

A Chewsday.

The white-eyed moray eel gets its name from the fact that it has white irises.

KNOCK, KNOCK.

Who's there?
Ken.
Ken who?
Ken I come in?
It's freezing out here.

Say this fast three times:

Shorn sheep sleep soundly.

Adult female sheep are called ewes, males are called rams, and babies are called lambs. There are more than 1 billion sheep on Earth!

KNOCK, KNOCK.

Who's there?
Bison.
Bison who?
Bison, Mommy is off to work now.

A cat can jump about five times its own height.

190

Q What do you call a super-cool rodent?

A An awesome possum.

Q Why don't **bicycles** like to get up **early?**

A Because they are two tired.

Q What do you get if a **baker** turns into a **zombie?**

A Night of the Living Bread.

ANNA: Hey, how did you enjoy the seven-day Sausage Festival?

STEPHEN: It was the wurst week!

Q

Who did the **mortician** invite to his **party?**

Anyone he could dig up.

A

Say this fast three times:

Babette bought blackberries. Bert bought blueberries.

Q What side of a zebra has the most stripes?

A The outside.

Q

What do you call **horses** that go out **after dark?**

Nightmares.

A

Gorillas are the world's largest primates. A mature male can weigh 300 to 500 pounds (136 to 227 kg).

KNOCK, KNOCK.

Who's there?
Wafer.
Wafer who?
You've been a wafer so long!

193

When frightened, the frilled lizard fans out the ruffled spines around its neck to make itself look bigger.

KNOCK, KNOCK.

Who's there?
Whittle.
Whittle who?
I'm running a whittle bit late.

KNOCK,

KNOCK.

Who's there?
Finkle.
Finkle who?
Finkle go for a drive,
want to come?

A gray wolf can eat up
to 20 pounds (9 kg) of
food in one meal!

NINA:
Have you seen my potatoes?

DAVID:
No, but I will keep my eyes peeled.

TONGUE
TWISTER!

Say this fast three times:

Maggie made magnificent mudpies.

Say this fast three times:

Listen to the local yokel yodel.

Q What do you get if you put a kangaroo in the freezer?

A A hop-cicle.

Q What do **wasps** take to feel **healthy?**

A Vitamin Bee.

What kind of **dog** lives in a **hair salon?**

A Shampoodle.

Pigs have an excellent sense of smell. They use their snouts to find food in the ground.

201

JOKEFINDER

Tongue Twisters

ILLUSTRATIONCREDITS

Credit Abbreviations:
SS: Shutterstock

Cover: © Martin Harvey/SuperStock; 4–5 Cre8tive Images/SS; 6 Neale Cousland/SS; 7 (up), dwori/SS; 7 (bottom), pedalist/SS; 8 (bottom, left), Cornelia Anghel/SS; 8 (top, left), Gelpi JM/SS; 8 (top, right), Tsekhmister/SS; 8 (top, right), Andrew Buckin/SS; 9 Vitaly Titov & Maria Sidelnikova/SS; 10–11 Vinciber/SS; 12 (bottom), Iliuta Goean/SS; 12 (top), anyamuse/SS; 13 Coronado/SS; 14 alvant/SS; 14 (top, left), Moises Fernandez Acosta/SS; 14 (top, left), Jeehyun/SS; 15 (bottom, left), Jason Prince/SS; 15 (bottom, right), Svetlana Larina/SS; 15 (bottom, right), Lasse Kristensen/SS; 15 (top, left), Nito/SS; 15 (top, left), Brooke Becker/SS; 15 (bottom, left), Filipw/SS; 16 Eric Isselee/SS; 16 (top, left), Kruglov_Orda/SS; 17 (bottom, right), fivespots/SS; 17 (top, left), fivespots/SS; 17 (top, right), Eric Isselee/SS; 18 Ang Toon Yew/SS; 19 ra3rn/SS; 20 (bottom, left), vovan/SS; 20 (bottom, right), Sashkin/SS; 20 (top, left), Elena Schweitzer/SS; 20 (top, left), Wiktory/SS; 21 Richard Bowden/SS; 22–23 Eric Isselee/SS; 24 Iakov Kalinin/SS; 25 (bottom, left), Art_girl/SS; 25 (bottom, right), Alenavlad/SS; 25 (top, left), nikkytok/SS; 26 (bottom, right), EcoPrint/SS; 26 (top, left), DenisNata/SS; 26 (top, right), vadim kozlovsky/SS; 26 (top, right), Foonia/SS; 27 karamysh/SS; 28–29 Bjorn Stefanson/SS; 29, (top, right), Aquir/SS; 30 Joy Brown/SS; 31 (bottom), Ijansempoi/SS; 31 (bottom), Verock/Shutterstock; 32 (bottom, left), KAMONRAT/SS; 32 (top, left), Eric Isselee/SS; 32 (top, left), Daniela Pelazza/SS; 32 (top, right), Stockagogo, Craig Barhorst/SS; 32 (top, right), pzAxe/SS; 33 Stepan Jezek/SS; 34–35 Eric Isselee/SS; 36 Volodymyr Burdiak/SS; 36 (top), Elena Schweitzer/SS; 37 (bottom, left), Michel Cecconi/SS; 37 (bottom, left), Dmitry Kalinovsky/SS; 37 (bottom, right), Petr Malyshev/SS; 37 (top, left), Iryna Rasko/SS; 37 (top, right), Maks Narodenko/SS; 37 (top, right), Natykach Nataliia/SS; 38 Andresr/SS; 39 Stephen Lavery/SS; 40–41 majeczka/SS; 40 (bottom), Eric Isselee/SS; 42 Anan Kaewkhammul/SS; 43 (bottom, left), Studio 1231/SS; 43 (bottom, right), BGSmith/SS; 43 (top, left), Graphic design/SS; 43 (top, left), Dmytro Pylypenko/SS; 43 (top, right), Keith Publicover/SS; 44 Robynrg/SS; 45 Leena Robinson/SS; 46–47 Eric Isselee/SS; 48 (bottom, right), Kavun Kseniia/SS; 48 (top, left), stock creations/SS; 48 (top, right), talseN/SS; 49 Eric Isselee/SS; 49 (bottom, right), gbreezy/SS; 49 (top, right), Nejron Photo/SS; 50 Brian Lasenby/SS; 51 (bottom, left), Robert Spriggs/SS; 51 (bottom, left), DM7/SS; 51 (top, left), studioVin/SS; 51 (top, left), Volodymyr Burdiak/SS; 52–53 Erik Lam/SS; 53 (bottom), 3dfoto/SS; 54 David Young/SS; 55 (top, right), Andrey Eremin/SS; 55 (top, right), Maks Narodenko/SS; 56 (bottom, right), Beth Shepherd Peters/SS; 56 (top, left), John Carnemolla/SS; 57 Tsekhmister/SS; 57 (top), Mark52/SS; 58–59 Eric Isselee/SS; 60 Nagel Photography/SS; 61 (bottom, left), Four Oaks/SS; 61 (bottom, left), Preto Perola/SS; 61 (bottom, right), Smit/SS; 61 (top, left), Studio 1One/SS; 62 S.P./SS; 63 red-feniks/SS; 64–65 Tony Campbell/SS; 65 Adisa/SS; 66 Cuson/SS; 67 (bottom), ollyy/SS; 67 (top), Cousin_Avi/SS; 68 (bottom, left), MSPhotographic/SS; 68 (bottom, right),JMiks/SS; 68 (bottom, right), irin-k/SS; 68 (top, right), Ljupco Smokovski/SS; 69 Jacqueline Perez/Dreamstime; 69 (bottom), Oleg Belov/SS; 70 Stanislav Duben/SS; 71 (bottom, left), oksana2010/SS; 71 (bottom, left), Ian 2010/SS; 71 (bottom, right), Greenland/SS; 71 (bottom, right), Aaron Amat/SS; 72–73 Eric Isselee/SS; 74 (bottom, left), Brittny/SS; 74 (bottom, right), photastic/SS; 74 (bottom, right), Crepesoles/SS; 74 (bottom, right), Andrey Eremin/SS; 74 (top, left), Richard Peterson/SS; 74 (top, left), Peter Zijlstra/SS; 74 (top, left), Moises Fernandez Acosta/SS; 75 Krzysztof Wiktor/SS; 75 (top), Chiyacat/SS; 76–77 Elena Schweitzer/SS; 78 Reinhold Leitner/SS; 79 (bottom), Aga & Miko (arsat),/SS; 79 (top), Eric Isselee/SS; 80 (bottom, left), Elena Elisseeva/SS; 80 (top, left), Steve Collender/SS; 80 (top, left), Steve Oehlenschlager/SS; 80 (top, right), Pixsooz/SS; 81 Jose Gil/SS; 82–83 Eric Isselee/SS; 84 Jacqueline Abromeit/SS; 85 (bottom, left), ericlefrancais/SS; 85 (bottom, left), avian/SS; 85 (top, left), Lightspring/SS; 85 (top, right), Dudarev Mikhail/SS; 86 (bottom), Mehmetcan/SS; 86 (top), Sutsaiy/SS; 87 Steve Noakes/SS; 88–89 Olga Popova/SS; 90 Bierchen/SS; 90 (bottom), Maglara/SS; 91 (bottom, left), Grauvision/SS; 91 (bottom, right), jareynolds/SS; 91 (top, right), DimkaSL/SS; 92 (bottom, left), Lena Pantiukh/SS; 92 (bottom, left), photovs/SS; 92 (bottom, right), Lori Labrecque/SS; 93 (bottom, right), Ozja/SS; 93 Patryk Kosmider/SS; 94–95 Eric Isselee/SS; 96–97 Happetr/SS; 98 Ermess/SS; 99 (bottom), Johan W. Elzenga/SS; 99 (top), Fer Gregory/SS; 100 (top, left), Andrei Shumskiy/SS; 100 (top, right), Ivonne Wierink/SS; 101 iolya/SS; 102–103 Tassel78/SS; 103 (bottom, left), Photastic/SS; 103 (right), SAYAM TRIRATTANAPAIBOON/SS; 104 Kellie L. Folkerts/SS; 105 (bottom, right), AR Images/SS; 105 (top, left), gualtiero boffi/SS; 105 (top, left), MilousSK/SS; 106 (bottom, right), John Wollwerth/SS; 106 (top, left), simongaberscik/SS; 107 Pavel L Photo and Video/SS;

Published by the National Geographic Society
John M. Fahey, Jr., *Chairman of the Board and Chief Executive Officer*
Declan Moore, *Executive Vice President; President, Publishing and Travel*
Melina Gerosa Bellows, *Executive Vice President; Chief Creative Officer, Books, Kids, and Family*

Prepared by the Book Division
Hector Sierra, *Senior Vice President and General Manager*
Nancy Laties Feresten, *Senior Vice President, Kids Publishing and Media*
Jay Sumner, *Director of Photography, Children's Publishing*
Jennifer Emmett, *Vice President, Editorial Director, Children's Books*
Eva Absher-Schantz, *Design Director, Kids Publishing and Media*
R. Gary Colbert, *Production Director*
Jennifer A. Thornton, *Director of Managing Editorial*

Staff for This Book
Kate Olesin, *Project Editor*
David Seager, *Art Director*
Lisa Jewell, *Photo Editor*
Ariane Szu-Tu, *Editorial Assistant*
Callie Broaddus, *Design Production Assistant*
Hillary Moloney, *Associate Photo Editor*
Grace Hill, *Associate Managing Editor*
Joan Gossett, *Production Editor*
Lewis R. Bassford, *Production Manager*
Susan Borke, *Legal and Business Affairs*

Production Services
Phillip L. Schlosser, *Senior Vice President*
Chris Brown, *Vice President, NG Book Manufacturing*
George Bounelis, *Vice President, Production Services*
Nicole Elliott, *Manager*
Rachel Faulise, *Manager*
Robert L. Barr, *Manager*

Editorial, Design, and Production by Plan B Book Packagers

CELEBRATING
‹125›
YEARS

The National Geographic Society is one of the world's largest nonprofit scientific and educational organizations. Founded in 1888 to "increase and diffuse geographic knowledge," the Society's mission is to inspire people to care about the planet. It reaches more than 400 million people worldwide each month through its official journal, *National Geographic*, and other magazines; National Geographic Channel; television documentaries; music; radio; films; books; DVDs; maps; exhibitions; live events; school publishing programs; interactive media; and merchandise. National Geographic has funded more than 10,000 scientific research, conservation and exploration projects and supports an education program promoting geographic literacy.

For more information, please visit www.nationalgeographic.com, call
1-800-NGS LINE (647-5463), or write to the following address:
National Geographic Society
1145 17th Street N.W.
Washington, D.C. 20036-4688 U.S.A.

Visit us online at nationalgeographic.com/books

For librarians and teachers: ngchildrensbooks.org

More for kids from National Geographic: kids.nationalgeographic.com

For information about special discounts for bulk purchases, please contact National Geographic Books Special Sales: ngspecsales@ngs.org

For rights or permissions inquiries, please contact National Geographic Books Subsidiary Rights: ngbookrights@ngs.org

Paperback ISBN: 978-1-4263-1378-3
Reinforced Library Binding ISBN: 978-1-4263-1379-0
Scholastic ISBN: 978-1-4263-1820-7

Printed in China

14/PPS/2